Take Your Hat Off, Son!

Charles Simpson

Illustrated by Joe McCormick

ISBN 1-58169-073-8
For Worldwide Distribution
Printed in the U.S.A.

Published by:
Evergreen Press
P.O. Box 191540 • Mobile, AL 36619
800-367-8203

In cooperation with
CSM Publishing
P.O. Box Z
Mobile, AL 36616

Table of Contents

Dedication

To Bob Terrell and John Norwood
who both loved to hear
and to tell a good story.

Introduction

I was licensed to minister in 1955, ordained in 1957, and since 1964 have traveled all over the U.S. and many countries. It has been my privilege to speak to attentive and supportive people many, many times.

I've always been surprised at what people remember and what they don't remember. One thing I've learned is people remember the stories. Perhaps it's because when you tell a story their mind becomes a screen upon which you project images. The stories stay with them as they use their imagination. No doubt each person is hearing and seeing the story a little differently. But they remember it.

I, too, love a good story. My father was a minister and he both told and enjoyed good stories. My grandfather was a Baptist deacon, and he, too, loved good stories. My father grew up listening to stories long before television came into being. In fact, he told me about the first crystal radio sets that they listened to and how they used to gather around it. Stories were a big part of the entertainment of those days and people used their imagination both to tell and to hear a good story. In fact, storytelling became a real art; an art that was preserved in the Old South for a long time and it still exists to some extent to this day.

The Bible is a book of stories, and history is called, "His Story." In ancient times, stories were passed along as a means of preserving history. People remembered them. They practiced the art of listening as well as telling stories and passing them on to their children. Hence we have history through stories.

As a minister, I learned early on that the way to leave a message with people was to tell a story. Not only a biblical story, but also stories which supported the biblical plot. So I began to take note of stories, some that I heard my father or some other minister tell or stories that I read.

I was about nine years old when my father and I were driving down a south Louisiana road in bayou country and he told me, "Son, there's a story in everything if you can just find it." I remember looking out on the field that was beside the road and just behind it was the thick swamp, wondering, *What is the story out there?* It impressed me so much that I began to look at things as having a story and extracting from those things the story that made it a thing of interest and even, perhaps, it held a moral lesson.

It was my father's training that caused me to begin to look for stories. I have had my wife tell me "Charles, you and I can be in the same situation and later when you describe it, it is different than I remembered it." It's not that she was saying that I was dishonest in describing it but rather that I had seen something that she did not see. I'm sure it's because I was trained to look for it. No doubt I have missed many many stories and forgotten some that I had learned. But I've come to appreciate a story.

Most of the stories in this little book are humorous stories. I learned early that it is good to laugh and to make others laugh. I've learned since that it's a great power to bring people joy. For many years as a minister, I did not fully realize how important it was to lift people's spirits. Too often my messages left people somewhat depressed. I thought Jesus said to Peter, "Beat my sheep." I found it later that He said, "Feed my sheep." I hope these stories feed you.

Growing Up

One Sunday afternoon began with great promise. I went with my father to a "dinner on the grounds" (an outdoor potluck meal) at a local, small town church about 6 or 7 miles from the church where he pastored.

I was 16 years old and had recently received my driver's license—a momentous occasion for any young man, but especially so for those of us with driving fever. I attended the dinner not only to enjoy the good food, but also, hopefully, to use the car while he was conducting an afternoon meeting. I planned to visit some of my friends who lived not too far away. After lunch, I approached my dad. Mind you, I was 16 and really wanted to get my hands on the wheel of the car. My dad really didn't want me to drive...I could tell. But I had him in a corner in front of all the other people, and I pressed him. I said, "Dad, I want to use the car. I won't be too long."

Finally, he relented and handed me the keys. I felt like I had been anointed high priest or something whenever he gave them to me. With a great sense of accomplishment, I headed toward the car. I was wearing a little brown corduroy hat, cocked over on the side of my head. I liked hats. I had several different kinds. I had engineer's hats, army fatigue hats, baseball hats, and sailor hats. I had so many of them that frequently I'd see someone walking down the road with a hat like one of mine and quickly realize that my mother had given another one of them away.

Before we left home that day, I had proudly put on my little corduroy brown hat in anticipation of using the family car. I was 16 years old and had the keys to our '52 Chevy in my hands. I slipped into the front seat of our black, plain, country preacher's car. Although it had no snazzy chrome or whitewall tires, it was a car. After cranking it up, I started backing it out of the parking lot. I turned the wheels and, to my chagrin, the right front wheel went off into a culvert. I felt a jolt, and then I was stuck. There were about 200 people over by the tables eating lunch and watching my sad performance…and there was my dad watching me make a fool of myself. Everyone saw what had happened…including him.

My dad was a fair complected sandy-haired man and sometimes he would look like a thermometer. His face would start to get red and the color would go right up to the top of his head, like it did that day. I was greatly embarrassed. Several fellas came over and picked up the front end of the car and helped me out of the culvert. But as I continued backing up, I suddenly realized that the car wouldn't steer. I had broken the front tie rod. There I was, sitting behind the now useless steering wheel with my brown corduroy hat cocked on my head, and all those people staring at me. When my dad began walking toward me, I wondered what he was going to say. I always wondered what dad was going to say when I had done something really stupid. He just stood there and looked at me as the

people gathered around. He said simply, "Take your hat off, son." That's all he said, but he might as well have said, "Take off your clothes." I felt totally undressed in front of everybody. (Of course, later at home he had much more to say to me….)

———✦◆✦———

Country stores in the old days were very small. They seemed quite large to me at the time, but usually they were not much bigger than two or three ordinary rooms in a house. Quite often people would actually live in two or three rooms in the same building, so it was called a "storehouse." My mother's parents ran such a store in southern Louisiana.

When I was about seven years old, our family lived in southern Alabama, and we had a store just behind our house. For me, a trip to the store meant going through my backyard and through their backyard and around to the front where I entered the store. I remember on one occasion going in and seeing an old

3

man in overalls looking kind of poorly. He was saying to the clerk who was also the wife of the owner, "I run out of chewing tobacco the other day and I tried some of my wife's snuff. But I been sort of sick ever since." Now it didn't strike me as all *that* funny. But I went home and told my mother what I had heard, and she thought it was very funny and laughed a lot. More than the story, the fact that my mother thought it was funny impressed me. It made me feel good to make Mama laugh.

———————

When I was in the fourth grade, I was in the 4-H club. We used to all go to the community hall (which was part of the school campus) for 4-H club meetings. And we especially liked it because we got out of class. They discussed different things, mostly things that pertained to farming people. My dad was a preacher, but most of the folks in the community were dependent on farming for their livelihood, so we all took an interest in agriculture.

During the 4-H club meeting, they would often give people an opportunity to tell a joke. One day, I remembered a joke that my dad told us at home, and so I got up and shared the following story with them:

As two men were going across the field, an angry bull approached them. When they finally saw him, he was snorting and pawing the ground. He quickly went chasing after them. They ran as hard as they could to the edge of the woods. One of the men ran up a tree, and the other one ran into a hole in the ground. When

4

the bull would charge the tree, the man would come out of the hole, and then the bull would change directions and charge the man on the ground, and he would run back into the hole. Then the bull would again charge the tree, and the situation would repeat itself. This went on until the man in the tree shouted to his friend on the ground, "You fool! Stay in the hole."

The man emerging from the hole shouted back, "I'm no fool. There's a bear in this hole!"

Now everybody laughed. The fact is, once again, I didn't think that the joke was *that* funny, but I enjoyed making the other people laugh. I never will forget that joke even though that's been many, many years ago. One reason I remember it is because people thought it was funny.

That was just one of many stories that I remember my dad telling with great enjoyment. I fondly remember Dad laughing. When Dad laughed, he laughed with real gusto. You could hear him quite a distance away. He was a gregarious, outgoing person who enjoyed laughter to its fullest extent. His laughter made the joke even funnier. People always enjoyed laughing with him.

The year I turned 17 was the worst year of my life. (Even worse than 16 when I started driving legally.) I developed a strong sense of independence and a streak of rebellion. On top of that, the Lord was dealing with me about being a minister, which was about last on my list of things to do. I grew up a preacher's kid and lived in a pastorium right next to the church. A pastorium is sort of like an aquarium except it's where churches keep pastors. It was a country church. There were good folks in the town, and it was a great place to grow up. But I rebelled against being a minister's son, let alone being a minister. I didn't like the fact that the church voted publicly on my daddy's salary, which was hardly worth voting on anyway, and I especially hated living in that goldfish bowl.

I also didn't care for the fact that my dad always drove a plain, 4-door Chevrolet or Ford. One time my dad bought a red Pontiac in 1946 right after the war, and it caused him no end of trouble in the community because they said he was making too much money. So I had it figured out that I was going to be an attorney. (My brother intended to become a preacher but wound up being an attorney, and I wound up being the preacher.) The Lord was dealing with me because my parents had given me to God when I was born. I was the first-born, and they held me up to the Lord and dedicated my life to Him. Later on, I wondered why they didn't wait and ask me if I wanted them to do that. They firmly believed that the first-born belonged to God, and so they gave me to Him.

When I was 17, the Lord came around to collect, but I had no intention of letting Him. I was not about to become a minister. I thought maybe if I could become successful and give a good tithe, I'd help God out a lot more. Nobody suspected that I was going to be a preacher anyway—I wasn't acting like one at all. Among my bad habits was coming in late, usually on Saturday night when my daddy needed his rest to get ready for Sunday. I was totally insensitive to the needs of a preacher. (Of course, later on when I had my own kids and needed to prepare for Sunday services, I became very sensitive to it.) It was Daddy's custom to leave the car out front. If I were without my friends when I came in, I would put the car away for him. I had graduated to having my own keys by then. I would rev the car up and whip it up around the corner of the house and down the driveway right into the garage. Just as the front end entered the garage, I'd hit the brakes and slide right up against the back wall.

One night I came in later than usual. I was not in good shape, and it was really dark outside because there was no moon. What I didn't know was that my dad had prepared for a Vacation Bible School parade that they were having in the community by borrowing some brand new loudspeakers from a friend. He had mounted them on top of the car, but they were black so I couldn't see them in the darkness (especially in my condition). I revved the car up as I usually did and started around the corner of the house. Just as I got to the garage and slammed down on the brakes, those loudspeakers smashed into the top of the garage. It sounded like thunder. The roof of the car caved in and the loudspeakers bounced off the trunk and flew out into the yard. It was sudden and complete destruction!

At first, I thought God had finally gotten tired of

me and just decided to kill me. When I managed to get out of the car, I could see what had happened because my father turned on all the lights in the backyard. The crash had shaken my parents up pretty badly too, although my dad probably figured out pretty quickly what I had done. Suddenly I thought, *Oh Lord! He's going to shoot me. He's getting his gun right now. He's had enough of me, and he's just going to come out here and shoot me.* I knew he'd be mad…real mad. Well, he hurried out the backdoor, looked at all of it, and saw me in my condition. In fact, I was so nervous I could only speak in falsetto. Here I was—a 17-year-old who up until a few minutes before thought he was pretty tough, but now I was scared to death and had a voice like a soprano. My dad looked at the debris in the yard and over at the car with its roof bent in and the smashed-in trunk. He walked up to me, put his arm around my shoulder, and said, "Son, it looks like you're still climbing fool's hill." I replied, "Yeah, I reckon so, Dad."

My dad believed in work, and he believed that as soon as you were old enough you ought to earn your pay. I had chores around the house from about the time I was seven years old. One of my chores was pulling down the shades. In those days, shades weren't like they are now—they were spring-loaded. Sometimes they worked, and sometimes they didn't. My dad had a phobia about when it got dark—the shades always had to be down. He did not want to lose the privacy of the family, so he didn't want people driving down the road and looking into our house. He figured when the lights came on, the shades came down, and that he designated to be my job. If they weren't down, there was usually some punishment involved. Well, sometimes I pulled the shades down, but if I pulled them too far down they would stick. Or if I didn't get them set just right, they would flap back up. I remember some spankings over those shades, but he drilled it into me that the shades ought to be down at dusk. To this day, if I walk in my house, the blinds have to be pulled when the lights go on. In fact, if I go into your house after dusk, and the shades are not down, I will probably pull them down or close the drapes just out of pure habit.

When I became a little older, I moved beyond just pulling down the shades. I had a job at the school sweeping the classrooms. Of course, you can't do that any more nowadays because of various rules and regulations. But at that time, I was making six cents a room—pretty good money for a nine year old. You could buy a Popsicle with six cents, and I was sweeping five or six rooms every afternoon. Some of my friends got the idea that we ought to strike for seven cents. That didn't go over well, and we all got fired. That was a sad day for me, and I learned a lot about management and labor relations.

When I was ten years old, my dad thought I needed to go on out and get another job. He said, "If you don't, I am going to cut off your allowance." I didn't get a job right away, and he held true to his word. Then I "felt led" to go out and look for a way to earn some money. When I was 11, I got a job stocking groceries in a local grocery store. The manager promised to pay me $3 for each Saturday's work. But when I got my check, it was only $2.40 because he had to take out 60¢ for social security and income tax. That cut represented about 20 percent of my pay! I argued with him about it, but he said the government made him do it. So I learned to hate the government when I was 11 years old. But I had another problem. I went home and asked my dad about tithing.

"Dad, do you tithe on the net or the gross?" was my question.

It would make a six-cent difference whether I tithed on the entire $3 or on the $2.40, which is what I took home. I thought my dad would give me a straight answer. After all, six cents would buy a Popsicle. But my dad didn't.

He said, "Son, do what's in your heart."

Well, I didn't want the Lord to know what was in my heart, so I went on and gave the whole 30¢. But I learned a big lesson and conquered the issue when the difference was only 6¢, which helped me later on when I earned much more money than that. I have tithed all my life. I believe in tithing so much that if I backslid, I'd mail it in. Some folks worry that the Lord will come back and catch them in a bar or some such place. I worry that He would come back and catch me with His money in my pocket.

Of course, I did eventually commit my life to be a minister. I'll tell you what finally did it. I was singing in the choir when I was 18 years old. I don't know if I had any business being in the choir, but I was in it during a series of revival meetings. The Lord was sorely dealing with me and had been for two years. I figured that after all my experiences, if I didn't eventually go on and follow through on the dedication my parents had made and on what I believed the Holy Spirit was saying to me, that God just might kill me. And so on this particular night the conviction was getting pretty strong, so I made a deal with the Lord at the close of the meeting.

I said, "Well, if they sing 'Just As I Am' one more time (which was highly unlikely because they had sung it right on off the page), and if Elton Tanner comes forward, I'd go on down and commit myself to be a minister. (Elton Tanner was a couple of years older than me and played football on our team. He lived several miles away and ordinarily attended another church.) Elton didn't even live in our community; I wasn't sure why he was visiting our church that night; perhaps it was because of the revival. But I said, "Lord, if they sing that song just one more time, and Elton Tanner comes forward tonight, I will go down." I figured there was as much chance of that happening as the backdoor walking on down the aisle.

Then my father, the pastor, said, "Now we're going to sing 'Just As I Am' just one more time." I thought that was only half the deal. But as soon as he said that,

Elton Tanner started walking down the aisle. Well, I beat him to the front because I was in the choir. I thought that God would kill me right there if I didn't move.

My dad asked me, "Why did you come forward?"

"I am dedicating my life to be a minister," I told him.

My dad said, "Praise the Lord!" I thought to myself, *Why?*

Everybody seemed glad for all the decisions that night. But when they came up to me, they looked at me strangely because they didn't know whether I would follow through on my promise. But I did and went on off to college to become a minister. At first, I didn't want to tell people that's what I was preparing for. I would tell them that I was going to be a teacher or that I was studying philosophy or something. I was embarrassed at the entire idea.

———————

In my second year of college, I transferred from Southern Mississippi University (now the University of Southern Mississippi) to what was then Howard College in the eastern part of Birmingham, Alabama (later it became Samford University). I got a job, as usual, working in a meat market in the Bessemer section of town where our customers were predominately black folks. It was late one Friday night and my first weekend in this particular market. I was trying to clean up the place and close it when a rather large, gregarious black lady came in the front door. When you're trying to close a store, it happens more often than not that someone comes in who wants to shop around or talk. I knew this lady would eventually make it back to the meat counter, which she did. She was a jovial person.

She said, "You're new around here, ain't you?"

I replied, "I am."

"Do you go to school?"

"Yes, I go to Howard College."

"What are you studying?"

"I'm studying to be a preacher."

She just laughed out loud. Everyone could hear her. She said, "Boy, you don't study to be no preacher. Either you is or you ain't!"

Her words found their way into my heart, and I knew that the truth was, I was going to be a preacher. That's what I was, and I had to get over my embarrassment about that. It was the will of God. It was what was right. And I needed to make up my mind what I was going to be. But it didn't come easy.

Ministers

Because I grew up in church and later became a pastor, I enjoy church humor. One time there was a lady who had a little son about five years old. The pastor was about to pay them a visit, and the lady wanted everything to be just right. This pastor happened to have an extremely large nose. The lady was conscious of the fact that her five-year-old might make an innocent, but inappropriate comment about that fact. And so she warned him, "Son, the Reverend is coming to see us, and he has a large nose. Now, I don't want you to say anything about his nose. If you do, you're going to get a spanking."

He promised her, "I won't say anything about it."

Shortly afterwards, a knock came at the door. The lady ushered the Reverend into the dining room and they sat down. Politely, she offered the minister some coffee, and he gratefully accepted. She noticed her son staring up at the minister's nose. She was sure that at any moment he was going to say something about it. So she said, "Reverend, will you excuse us for a moment?"

He graciously replied, "Why, sure."

She took her son into the kitchen and told him, "If you say anything about the Reverend's nose, you're going to get a licking!"

Again reassuring her, he said, "I'm not going to say anything, Mama."

So they proceeded back into the dining room, and the lady poured the Reverend a cup of coffee.

She asked him, "Reverend, do you like sugar with your nose?"

———◆✳◆———

There's a story about a minister who wanted to raise money for a building program, so he wired the pews and had buttons in the pulpit. He knew where everyone habitually sat, and he could pretty much guess how people ought to be giving. So whenever he called for a $100 contribution, he would say, "How many of you will give $100?" and he would press a button in the pulpit and those in the corresponding seats would jump up, and he would accept their commitments. He also had a $50 button and a $25 button. It worked pretty well until a Scotsman showed up at church, and he electrocuted him. (I can tell that story because our ancestry is Scot/Irish, though we never were that close with a dollar.)

15

Some people take themselves too seriously, especially some preachers. My dad used to tell a story about two Baptist preachers who went off to a convention. One of them had good eyesight but was rather sanctimonious. The other one was blind but had a good sense of humor. Since it was such a large convention, all the restaurants were crowded, and it was hard to find a place to eat. The only suitable place they could find was at a subterranean restaurant. So they went downstairs into this basement type restaurant, and it was rather dark down there. Of course, the blind man couldn't see, and at first, the man who had sight couldn't see because of the contrast to the bright daylight outside. The blind man was hanging onto his arm, and they were both stumbling. The waitress thought they were drunk, so she said to them, "Shame on you two men, down here in the middle of the day drunk. Don't you know there's a religious convention in town?"

Whereupon the sighted minister, who was very sanctimonious, drew himself up and said to the woman, "I will have you to know that we're not drunk, we're Baptist preachers."

The blind minister said to her, "Don't pay him any mind. Every time he gets drunk, he thinks he's a Baptist preacher."

———◆◆◆———

Sometimes it's hard for a preacher to get a sense of direction for his sermon. I remember a "Far Side" cartoon that pictured a group of hound dogs standing around barking excitedly and all ready for the hunt. There were some men standing nearby with guns. The lead dog was out front with his nose to the ground, saying to himself, "I can't smell a thing."

Sometimes it's like that in the ministry. Everybody is all fired up and eager to go, but the preacher is having trouble catching the scent for some kind of direction.

———◆✦◆———

One preacher got up and said to his congregation, "Today, I am not prepared. I am embarrassed to say it, but I am just going to have to trust the Holy Spirit to lead me. However, next Sunday, I hope I can do better."

———◆✦◆———

One nervous, young Presbyterian ministerial candidate was being examined by a group of stately old Elders, and they asked him a number of questions about his doctrine. Finally, one of them asked him the ultimate Calvinist question: "Young man, would you be willing to be accursed for the glory of God?"

The young man, wiping the perspiration off his forehead, looked relieved at the question and said, "Oh, yes sir! I would be willing for this entire Presbytery to be cursed for the glory of God."

———◆✦◆———

About 30 years ago, I was in Jamaica. There was a Jamaican lady there that had a great sense of humor. She told me that their church had lost its pastor. They sent across the island for a substitute pastor to come in. Nobody knew him or even what he looked like, but he was recommended by another church. He came in on the train, and several of them went down to the station and met him. A man got off the train, dressed in a black suit with a vest, a black bowler hat, and looked like a very dignified gentleman. They went over to him and said, "You must be Reverend So-and-so."

Surprised, he said, "No."

"Are you sure you're not a reverend?"

Irritated now, he repeated, "No, I am not."

They said, "You sure do look like a minister."

He said, "I have stomach trouble."

———◆◆◆———

Several years ago I performed a wedding ceremony that wasn't going very well at all. They had planned to take communion, but when I reached for the cup I realized that there was no wine in the goblet nor was there any bread on the plate. Of course, all of that was supposed to have been taken care of, but somehow slipped through the cracks in the business of the preparations. Fortunately we could fake the wine, but I didn't have bread. However, I found a large mint in my pocket, so I broke it in two and shared it with them. Prior to that, when they repeated their vows, the groom was supposed to say to her, "I give thee my enduring affection." Instead he said, "I give thee my enduring infection."

Years ago I had a friend who was a pastor in Pittsburgh. His name was Ronald McDonald. One of his parishioners was doing construction work at a McDonald's hamburger place. In the course of remodeling the place, he fell and sustained a concussion. The paramedics came and got him. As they were bringing him to the hospital, he told them, "Please call my pastor."

And they asked, "Who is your pastor?"

And yes, he *did* reply, "Ronald McDonald."

They didn't believe him of course, but the story made the front page of the Pittsburgh newspaper. Sometimes the truth is stranger than fiction.

Money

I heard about a $100 bill, a $50 bill, and a $1 bill that all went to heaven. The $100 bill said, "I had a great life. I went all over the world and saw some wonderful things." The $50 bill said, "I had a great life, too. I didn't go all over the world, but I did see a lot of wonderful things right here in the U.S.A." They turned to the $1 bill, and it said, "Well, I didn't go anywhere, and I didn't see anything, I was in church all my life."

A pastor friend said of his congregation, "They give 'til it hurts, but they have a very low pain threshold. A lot of them have an impediment in their reach. Some of them have shell-out falter, and a lot of them have sclerosis of the giver."

In recent history, many areas of the U.S. thought they could solve their financial problems by legalizing gambling. Back in the 1960s, my dad fought gambling. He was head of the pastors' committee in the area to stop gambling from coming into Mobile County, but a dog track came in anyway. Concerning gambling, he said, "You could make a small fortune gambling if you started with a large one."

A fellow drove his "piece of junk" to a garage and asked the mechanic what he thought it would take to fix it. The mechanic looked at it for a while and said, "My advice would be to keep the oil and change the car."

It might have been the same fellow who drove his car to a tollbooth, and the toll tender said, "75 cents." The man looked at him and said, "Sold!"

———◆·◆◆·◆———

A doctor and a lawyer got on an elevator one day, and the doctor said to the lawyer, "What do you do about people who see you on the street and always are asking you medical questions?

The lawyer said, "I would send them a bill."

The doctor said, "Thank you."

A couple of days later, the doctor got a bill from the lawyer.

———◆·◆◆·◆———

The man asked the lawyer, "How much do you charge?"

21

He said, "Well I'll answer a couple of questions for you for $500."

"That's kind of high, isn't it?" the man said.

The lawyer said, "Yes, and what's your second question?"

A sign on the front of a junkyard said, "We buy junk. We sell antiques."

Another sign said, "Why go elsewhere and get cheated when you can come here?"

Speaking of junk, a class had their 25th reunion, and the fellow who had been known as the class dunce showed up at the reunion driving a Mercedes. His beautiful wife was decked out in fine jewels and clothes. Someone asked him, "Aren't you the guy who flunked math?"

"Yes, I did," he answered.

"Well, you've done mighty well," they commented.

"Yes, I have."

"How did you do it?"

Proud as a peacock, he said, "I got into the junk business. And I found out that you could buy junk for $1 and sell it for $3. And that three percent just kept adding up!"

A farmer enjoyed poor health for many years and was, in fact, a hypochondriac. He made it a point to visit every new doctor who came into town. As he sat in the waiting room of the newest one, he noticed a sign that said, "$10 for the first visit; $7.50 for all visits thereafter."

So when he saw the doctor, he said, "I am glad to see you *again*, doctor."

The doctor said nothing but began to examine him. He tapped on his knee and listened to his chest and began to say, "Hmmm, hmmm." And then he got a real serious look on his face.

The farmer asked him, "What do I do, doctor?"

The doctor said, "You just keep doing the same thing I told you to do the first time."

———◆※◆———

One newly hired man, who was thrilled to finally obtain group insurance, became ill and had a costly office visit. Unfortunately, when he applied for reimbursement, he found out the whole group had to get sick before they would pay off.

———◆※◆———

Back in the 60s when I pastored a Baptist church, we had a family join the church. The father was a collector of silver dollars and had jars full of them. Some of his silver dollars were worth a good deal of money because they were rare. They had a son who had a problem with stealing. His son stole a large portion of those silver dollars and spent them at face value. What a loss!

A lot of times, people are taking things that God has given them without any realization of their true value. When we try and operate God's creation without God, we're not only stealing, but we're not able to use it to its fullest extent because we do not appreciate it.

———◆◆❂◆◆———

A minister friend told me this story. The mafia man was tired of being ripped off by his accountant so he hired a deaf mute to be his accountant, figuring that he wouldn't be talking to anybody and would be more trustworthy. Everything was fine until one day a million dollars was suddenly missing. The mafia don hired a sign language interpreter to come and talk to his accountant. He told the interpreter to ask the accountant where the missing money was. The interpreter signed to the mute, and the mute signed back, "I don't know."

The angry mafia man shouted, "You tell him that if he doesn't tell me where it is I am going to shoot him!"

And so the interpreter signed to the deaf mute, "He's going to shoot you."

The accountant quickly signed back, "The money is under the back steps at the warehouse."

The interpreter told the mafia don, "He said he doesn't know where your stupid money is."

It's a miracle that Columbus was so successful. He wasn't sure of his destination. He didn't know where he was most of the time or even where he had been. And he did it on somebody else's money.

Church

One fellow went to church and it was a really dead service. Afterwards, everybody went to the restaurant across the street to have something to eat. They were very friendly there. It was a lively place, just jumping with great fellowship. After his meal, the man was heard to say, "If this restaurant had membership, I believe I'd join it."

Another minister friend told me about a church that had become involved with renewal. Even though it had been really dead, when renewal came along, everybody still wasn't for it. The church became a little too exciting for some people—some of them began to say, "Amen" and even, "Hallelujah!" One of the sisters in the church complained, "If Jesus Christ knew what was going on in this church, He would turn over in His grave!"

My mother-in-law told me this story about another service that was really dead. Afterwards, the pastor wanted to liven it up a little bit, and so he said to all the members, "Go and introduce yourself to one of the guests. Shake hands with them and make them feel welcome."

There was one member, whose name was Gladys Dunne. She went over to one of the guests and said, "Hello, I'm Gladys Dunne."

The lady said, "I am, too!"

Gladys just walked away; she didn't know what else to say.

A lot of people have a habit of coming in and sitting on the back row. It fills up first and then the latecomers have to go all the way down front. So a pastor who was building a new church building, decided that he would cure that tendency. He just put one pew all the way across the back of the church. Whenever it filled up on Sunday morning, he hit a button and it slid down to the front and another one popped up in back.

I'm very grateful to be a believer in Jesus Christ, and I try to be a good Christian. Next to that I like a good football game—when it is right, you understand. I love a good Alabama/Auburn game, Mississippi State/Ole Miss game or Texas/A&M game. I even like a good Michigan/Michigan State game.

27

When I was in high school, I played football, and we had some very good teams. I played guard. Now a guard is a fullback with his brains kicked out. I wanted to be a quarterback, but I didn't have the equipment. Coach told me, "Simpson, you're little, but you are slow." He also said, "I swear you get smaller every game!"

Anyway, eventually I got into the ministry. Most ministers say that they got called. As you've heard, with me it was more like I got threatened. But that's a different story. I have learned to enjoy the Christian life. But I have sometimes thought that if football was like Christianity...

• Teams would be graded on their huddles, not wins and losses.

• Quarterbacks would make play calling more exciting.

• Teams would probably have music in the huddle.

• Unless players enjoyed the huddle, they wouldn't attend.

• Players would have the right to argue with the quarterback.

• Players would even sometimes get injured in the huddle.

• Coaches would spend more time counselling their players.

• If a player got injured on the field, his team-mates might finish him off.

• The purpose of the game would be less about advancing the ball, and more about whose ball it is.

28

• The rules would be whatever each team decided them to be. And teams could have no rules if they felt led.

Well, I'm glad football is not like church. It would spoil a good game. However, now if church was more like football...Amen!

I grew up around farms, and even worked on them from time to time. I pulled corn, dug potatoes, and such on Mr. Fletcher's farm, and later on I worked for Claude Jackson ("Mr. Claude" to me). He grew potatoes.

I have also wondered from time to time, what if farming was like Christianity? How would that affect the family farm?

• Farming would be more about barns than fields.

• Farmers would pretty much stay around the barn and have an office there.

• The best farmer would be the one with the biggest barn.

• Farmers would pray for it to rain *in* the barn and then pray for it to catch on fire.

• Farmers would both plow and plant inside the barn.

• Farmers would get voted out of the barn, similar to the T.V. program "Survivor."

• Farmers would look for a barn with no farmer in it.

• Because of all the activity inside barns, they would develop a bad odor.

• Due to the focus on the barn, the fields would grow more wild.

- Activity outside the barn would become more like hunting.

- Farmers would have more conventions, and while they were away, sometimes wild animals would come into the barn and cause havoc.

- The best farmers would be those who could give a sound talk about agriculture and use large words.

As I think about it, making farming more like Christianity would not be a sound idea. But now, if we made Christianity more like farming…Amen!

Not long after I became a minister, I served communion. I was 20 years old at the time, and I had not had a lot of practice. I made a mistake. I served the cup before the bread. When I realized I had served the cup first, I just went right on and did it as though that was the way you were supposed to do it. But one of the deacons, who was an older gentleman probably in his 60s, had taken communion so many times that he sensed something was different. Finally after the service, he put his finger on it. It hit him that I had served the cup first. He commented to me, "the bread goes before the cup." It seemed to make a real impact on him that we had gotten it out of order. I heard him mutter several times during the week, "The bread goes before the cup." It's unfortunate that habit so hypnotizes us that significance can be lost in form.

One pastor told his congregation, "As an example of penitence, I'm asking the whole church to worship during Lent in an unheated building. In other words, I'm asking us to give up heat for Lent."

As they left church, one parishioner asked another, "What do you plan to give up for Lent?"

The other parishioner said, "Church."

———◆◆◆◆———

Somewhere I read that there are signs telling you if you need to find another church. One is if there is a gun rack in the church van. Another is if the church staff consists of senior pastor, the socio pastor, the psycho pastor, and the humor pastor. Another sign is if the church uses the Dr. Seuss version of the Bible or if there's an ATM in the foyer. Another clue is if the usher asks you if you want to sit in the smoking or non-smoking section.

———◆◆◆◆———

Jesus called us all to be fishers of men. Some people think that a fisherman is a man with a license, or a man with a boat, or a man with good tackle. Actually a fisherman is a man with fish. We've got a lot of Christian fishermen who have a nice boat, a license, and good tackle, but they don't have any fish. So I guess they're really not fishermen.

Christian Growth

One minister wrote a sad parody on the hymn, "Onward, Christian Soldiers." His version went, "Like a mighty tortoise moves the Church of God, brothers we are trodding where we've always trod."

One pastor made a list of 357 sins mentioned in the Bible. Afterwards, he got many requests from people who were interested in obtaining the list. They were afraid that they had maybe missed one or two sins.

A lady came forward after the sermon and said, "Pastor I'm convicted about gossip, and I'd like to lay my tongue on the altar."

The pastor looked at the altar and said, "Well, get as much of it on there as you can."

I heard a fellow say one time that a lot of people grow up in church who are not Christians. He said growing up in church or hanging around the church doesn't mean you're a Christian any more than hanging around a garage makes you a car.

Scripture says, "Many are called but few are chosen." One minister said, "Many are cold, but a few are frozen.

Sonny Ellis was a businessman who served with me on the board of Integrity Music Co. established by Michael Coleman. Sonny was a good Baptist and a fine man. He said in my hearing one time that Christians were like teabags. They're not worth much unless they have been through hot water.

Adam didn't have drugs, alcohol, T.V., or movies, yet he still managed to sin. Maybe our environment isn't the entire problem.

———◆◈◆———

One parishioner asked her Baptist pastor, "Do you think Pentecostals will go to heaven?"

He said, "Why, I think they will if they don't run clear past it."

Deliverance

Years ago I was in a church that got heavily involved in getting people delivered from evil spirits. That was a new thing at the time, and it attracted a lot of attention. Folks came from all kinds of churches to see this phenomenon. Many people even came to the meetings who didn't believe in evil spirits, and others came who believed that you could have them alright, but never get rid of them. We had invited a well-known minister to the congregation to discuss the topic and provide some solutions.

Fortunately, I was ministering in a faraway country at the time, but I tried to prepare the church for what might happen. I told the elders of the church to be ready to pray for people who might be under the grip of some sort of evil spirit. I warned them that this minister who was coming was a very laid back fellow who didn't speak loud at all, and who had a real soft approach. But that didn't mean a thing because when he started praying, things were going to break out in the congregation—things that could become quite startling.

Well, the place was packed out with people standing around the back wall. The minister brought a very simple message about the existence of evil spirits and how they afflict people, and how to get rid of them. Then as he closed, he said he would ask God to

35

set people free. Well, sure enough, as soon as he started praying, people started "manifesting." There were some people who began to cry out, and it was bedlam. There was one minister sitting right next to a woman who actually started to scream. He had to cast an evil spirit out of her, and he didn't even believe in it.

Then of course there were people who ran down to the altar to get prayed for. Our elders were just shocked at the rapid-fire response and they went forward and began to pray for people. One elder was trying to deal with one woman who obviously was shaken and had some kind of presence bothering her. He said to her, (speaking to the spirit) "You spirit, what is your name?"

She replied back in a strange voice, "Lying."

And he said, "You lying spirit, are you telling me the truth?"

He was overheard making that remark and has never lived down the humor of it. Never trust a lying spirit to tell you the truth.

Some years later the same well-known minister was speaking in a large auditorium to hundreds of people on the same subject. At the close of his talk, about 300 people came forward asking for prayer. The minister asked me and several others to help him and led us into a large room adjacent to the auditorium. When he explained to those people how he would pray, and what might happen, I realized that I was in a roomful of people who needed deliverance. I also realized that there were less than a dozen to help us. The odds were not good.

Sure enough, the minister prayed a soft simple prayer at the close of which, he commanded various spirits to leave the people seeking prayer. It was...it was bedlam! A young woman nearby began shrieking. I had not sooner cast out a spirit of fear than I turned to see a stocky fellow swinging "haymakers." As I turned to walk in his direction, he slugged me across the side of my head. For an instant I went blank, then I realized that I had him on the floor and was sitting on him, glaring down at his face. Then I said, "I think I have the same spirit that you have, fella!"

Animals

Of course, it's easy to criticize but it's much harder to do something constructive. I remember a story about an old gentleman who was driving out in the country and came upon an old service station that still had a hand-cranked pump for the gas. So he pulled his car over to the pump, and the old man that ran the station put the pump in his tank and began to crank on it. The customer looked over not far away, and there was a hound dog sitting on his haunches just howling up a storm. The customer said to the old gentleman, "What's the matter with that dog?"

"He's sitting on a thorn," the old man explained.

"Why doesn't he move?" the perplexed man asked.

"It's easier to howl," he answered.

A lot of folks would rather howl than move.

People can get real hung up on how a thing is said and miss the whole point. Two guys were arguing about whether a chicken is sitting or setting when she's on the nest. And so they asked a farmer, "When a chicken is on the nest, do you say she's *sitting* on it or she's *setting* on it?"

He thought a moment and replied, "I don't really care. What I want to know is when she cackles, is she laying or lying?"

A lot of Christians like to run after what's "hot" in the Christian world. They remind me of a story of a man who raised hogs. He had a large pen at the edge of the woods. He taught the hogs to come by beating a stick on the tree. The hogs always knew it was feeding time. They'd come running across the lot to the trough. But he had to give it up because a woodpecker came along and almost ran the hogs to death.

Gary Browning, a pastor friend of mine said that he and some friends were praying for a family named Bird. One of the men led out as they held hands in a circle and said, "Lord, this prayer is for the Birds." It cracked all of them up, and they had trouble praying any more after that.

My dad used to say that anxiety is a mild case of atheism. Someone else said that anxiety is mental fly-paper. Sometimes you can get a fixation on something, and it becomes very destructive. Back in the 60s, my wife and I lived in a home that was not air-conditioned. Of course, it gets very hot during the summer in the South. We had a big fan that drew in air from outside. An open window was just above our bed. Every morning about five o'clock, a bluejay would come and land in a bush just outside our window. It would begin to scream loudly and wake us up, of course. It was most annoying.

One morning I got up and went around the house and saw that there was a cat in the bush, and the bluejay was screaming at the cat. And I thought, *You stupid blue jay. That cat's going to get you.* One morning, I didn't hear the bluejay, and sure enough, when I went around the side of the house to go to work, I saw bluejay feathers all over the ground. I thought about how that bluejay could have flown anywhere in South Alabama, Mississippi, or even Florida. But he got the cat on his mind, and every night he would find himself going toward that bush, and the cat would meet him there. I thought, *If the bluejay could have just gotten the cat off his mind, he could have lived and flown anywhere.*

His brain caught on a snag, and his mental hang-up killed him.

———◆◆◆◆———

One of the best illustrations of the grace of God is that after Noah built the ark, God let woodpeckers on board.

Somebody else said that it's not the size of the dog in the fight, but the size of the fight in the dog.

One man said the air around here is so bad that even the birds are coughing.

———◆◆◆◆———

One of my favorite stories that my dad told was about a veterinarian who had been called by the farmer to treat a horse. As he prepared to give the horse a pill, he took a tube and put the pill in the tube, put the tube in the horse's mouth, and got ready to blow. But the horse blew first.

———◆◆◆◆———

A long time ago, when our youngest son, Jonathan, was a small boy, I decided to take him to a petting zoo that was featured at our local mall. It was very interesting. They had different kinds of animals, and you could walk through the areas where the animals were kept. Among the animals were goats. In with the goats, oddly enough, was a Dalmatian. My

41

son and I bought corn and when we began to feed the goats, the Dalmatian was trying to get some just as if it was a goat. I watched him for awhile, and sure enough, he was acting like the goats. Finally I turned to the dog and I said, "Look, you're not a goat, you're a dog." He squatted on his haunches, cocked his head, and looked at me strangely as though someone had never told him that before.

I thought about it and realized that a lot of people run with the goats so much that they act just like them, but that is not how they were created to be. They don't know who they really are because they have just taken on the habits of the crowd they run with.

Bloopers

One of my minister friends is John Duke. He's been a friend of mine since 1966. We were having a convention one time and John was introducing a guest. Glen Basham was an outstanding young musician who played in the Detroit Symphony when he was about 20 years old. John wanted to give Glen a good introduction. So he listed some of Glen's accomplishments and finally said, "This is a young man who has certainly gone out and extinguished himself."

One minister called on a regular attendee to say the opening prayer. The member stood up and gave the benediction, so everybody left.

———◆◆◆———

I was getting ready to speak one time in Atlanta, Georgia, and a man whom I did not know was called upon to introduce me. It was a rather large gathering in a Methodist church. He went on and on about me even though I knew that he didn't know me that well. It wasn't very long before I realized that he had forgotten my name. Finally, he turned in a rather embarrassing way and asked, "Pastor, what is your name again?"

I remember another time in the same city when I was being introduced by a friend who intended to say that I had ministered widely across the U.S. Instead he said, "I want to present to you today a man who has ministered *wildly* across the U.S. (That probably was as accurate as the other way.)

———◆◆◆———

One person said to his pastor, "Pastor, your words are like water to a drowning man."

———◆◆◆———

Another man told his pastor, "Reverend, each one of your sermons is better than the next."

There's nothing quite so funny as people who take themselves very seriously when they make a mistake. At prayer meeting one Wednesday night, a lady stood up and requested prayer for a soap opera character who was having problems.

———•◦×◦•———

My dad told me about a man who returned from World War I. The hometown paper was going to play him up as a hero. They ran his picture and underneath it they ran this headline: "Bottle scarred veteran returns home." His relatives complained, and so they rewrote it: "Battle scared veteran returns home."

———•◦×◦•———

My dad used to tell about the times when trains were very popular and were considered luxurious modes of transportation long before people flew much in planes. A businessman was going east on a train that went through Chicago and finally on to Cleveland. He would be sleeping on a Pullman through the night, so he said to the porter, "I am a very hard sleeper. I've got to get off in Chicago in the middle of the night, and I want you to be sure that I am off this train. Now, I'll probably protest, and I may not want to get up, but here's $20. I want you to be very sure that I get off this train. I must close a big deal in Chicago tomorrow morning."

The porter said, "You're going to get off this train, don't you worry." And so he took the $20.

The next morning, the businessman woke up in Cleveland. He was extremely angry! He looked up the porter, rebuked him, and said a lot of unkind things. Finally, he got off the train. A bystander walked over to the porter and asked, "Why did you put up with all that man said? You didn't have to take all that."

The porter said, "If you think that man was mad, you should have seen the guy I put off in Chicago."

———◆◆◆◆———

Sometimes we try and say something, and it just doesn't come out right. A man was standing before a judge on trial for assault on another man.

The judge asked him, "Did you hit the man with a rock?"

He said, "Yes, Your Honor, I did."

"How big was the rock? As big as my fist?"

He said, "No, Your Honor, it was a little bigger than that."

"Was it as big as my two fists?"

"Yes, Your Honor, but it was even bigger than that."

"Well," the judge asked, "How big was it?"

He said, "Well, Your Honor, it was as big as your head, but not quite as thick."

———◆◆◆◆———

There was once a man who was eating in a restaurant and a young waiter asked him if he could ask him a riddle. So the man said, "Okay, what is it?"

He said, "My mother had a kid. It wasn't my brother or my sister. Who was it?"

The man thought awhile and said, "I give up."

The waiter said, "It was me."

The fellow laughed, and that evening he went home and told his wife that he had heard a good riddle.

"What is it?" she asked curiously.

"Well, my mother had a kid. It wasn't my brother or my sister. Who was it?"

After a few minutes, of thought, she said, "I give up."

He proudly said, "Some kid that I met downtown at lunch."

A newspaper article featured a photo of a local detective. It was captioned, "Detective on the police *farce*." They tried to correct it and wrote, "*Defective* on the police force."

There's a story about a rural pastor who proposed to his church that they buy a chandelier. One of the church members objected because he said, "There are three reasons: one, we don't have enough money; two, nobody can play it, and three, what this church really needs is lights."

In 1974 there was a horse named Basic Instinct. The horse was a 6-1 favorite to run at the Atlantic City racetrack, but he never ran because they closed the gate on the horse's tail.

In Tennessee, a workman's boot fell into a nuclear reactor and shut it down for 17 days.

On the U.S.S. Swordfish, a nuclear sub, a worker dropped a 50-cent paintbrush into a torpedo launcher, and it cost $171,000 to repair.

The Scripture says that it's the little foxes that eat the grapes.

Cars

One of the things that I always liked to do when I was young was to race cars. We never had a fast car, but I always did the best I could with whatever I had. I had a friend named Douglas Parker who liked to race as much as I did. His Daddy had a '51 Pontiac, and at that time, we had a '50 Plymouth. It wasn't very fast, but as I said, I did the best I could. One night during church, we both slipped out the back and headed out west of our little town on some paved rural highways, to race around awhile.

Finally, it was time to get back to church because they were going to be letting out. Unfortunately, I made a wrong turn and got lost. I was on a highway heading into Mobile and finally turned around. Now I knew I was going to be late. We were heading down a hill going as hard as we could go with the wind behind us.

It was dark, but I figured that the road went straight because there was a right-of-way cut through the woods. But it turned out to be a powerline right-of-way. As I reached the bottom of the hill, I suddenly saw that the road made an almost right angle turn. At the time, I was going wide open. The only thing I could do was to try and make the curve. However, it didn't have rack and pinion steering and was more like a bathtub on coil springs going down the road than a

49

race car. The car got right up on its side on the wheels and seemed like it stayed there for 30 minutes. I had a stupid thought come into my mind that I could reach out on the highway and strike a match, I was so close to the road. I knew that if that car ever started rolling it would never quit. It was lifting off the road. While it was in that condition between heaven and earth for what seemed like an eternity, the Lord spoke to me. He said, "Son, how would you like to be a minister?" I thought, *Dear God if the organ is playing, I'm ready to go down that aisle right now.* Finally I got the car stopped, but I couldn't work the pedals because my legs were too weak. Douglas came up behind me in the Pontiac, pulled over, and said, "Man, you scared me to death. I saw the whole underside of your car." I said, "It scared *you*...man, I was *in* the car." We were late and we "caught it" from our parents.

While I was "touched" by the Lord on that occasion, I wasn't through resisting Him. It took me about another year to come to the place where I was willing to say yes. But I learned something that if you're not going to repent, at least you better be careful. Of course that doesn't always work. I was in Mobile one night coming home thinking to myself, *I'd better be careful* because I wasn't living right. The road was a little bit slick due to a little drizzle. I was driving not more than 25 or 30 miles an hour when a lady in front of me in a much heavier car jammed on the brakes. I jammed on mine, but my front end dove and rode right up under her car. I don't think it did any damage to her car at all, but it tore up the grill on mine. It looked like I had been driving 50 mph. My father let me help pay for it....

------◆◆◆◆◆------

It seemed like when the Lord dealt with me He always used cars. One night I was racing down a rural highway, and I was coming up on U.S. 90; I decided that it was time to slow down. I passed some friends and waved at them and before I knew it, the highway was right in front of me. When I slammed on my brakes, I hit a little bit of pea gravel, and the car started sliding. It slid sideways and right across all four lanes of U.S. 90. I missed a Highway Patrol car by about 10 feet. It took me awhile to bring the car to a stop. The patrolman pulled up behind me, and when he got to my door, he was white as a sheet. He said,

"Son, I've got a boy about your age. If he did something like you just did, I would want to be sure to find out about it. I am going to be sure your daddy finds out about it." And he wrote me up a pretty big ticket.

Of course, my daddy did find out about it. I had to go before a Justice of the Peace who happened to be an elder in another church. He made me not only pay the fine, but come to see him several times, and we would sit down and talk about religion. He wanted to argue about falling from grace and whether you had to be baptized to be saved. As big a sinner as I was, I was willing to argue with him about it. We never solved that problem, but I did pay a big fine and spent a lot of time listening to an elder/Justice of the Peace. Of course the tough thing about paying the fine was that I had to do it with my own money.

One day I was driving down the road listening to National Public Radio, and they had a program that was entitled something like "University of the Air." They were having a classroom discussion. One of the students had presented a paper and was reading it to the class. In the course of his paper, he made a statement that read something like this: "My cousin was tinkering with the motor of his car."

The professor interrupted him and said, "That's incorrect."

"What do you mean, sir?" the student asked.

He said, "Well, when you said that your cousin

was tinkering *with* the motor of his car, 'with' implies that both he and the motor were tinkering. We know that the motor wasn't tinkering. He was tinkering." So the professor suggested several other possible prepositions. They tried saying that his cousin was tinkering "under" the motor. Well, that didn't work because it could meant that he just happened to be under the motor, but the tinkering had nothing to do with the motor. Then they decided they would do tinkering "on" the motor. But that was the same problem. He could have just been on top of the motor tinkering, but it wouldn't have had anything to do with the motor necessarily. So they finally decided that he was tinkering "at" the motor. I had to pull my car over I was laughing so hard because neither the student nor the professor were tinkering, it was his cousin. Probably neither one of them had ever tinkered with a motor at all. It was just an academic discussion. And so it is that a lot of people get all caught up in how a thing ought to be said when they haven't ever had any experience with it themselves.

Kids

A family was traveling by train in a Pullman car one night. The husband and wife were sleeping in a top bunk, and their little son who was about four years old was sleeping down below. The little boy was nervous because he had never slept on a train before. As they passed the crossings, he could see the lights flashing in the window and hear the bells ringing. He didn't want to go to sleep. In his little voice, he called up to the top bunk, "Dad, are you there?"

His dad said, "Yes, son. I'm here. Mama's here and God is here. Everything's okay." After a couple of minutes of silence, he thought the boy went to sleep.

About five minutes later, the same little voice asked, "Mama, are you there?"

She said, "Yes, son. Dad's here, and I'm here, and God's here. Everything's fine." She hoped that was an end to his questions.

Several minutes later, the little boy called out again, "Dad, are you there?"

By this time, a man who was sleeping on the other side of the thin partition was getting upset. He answered the little boy, "Yes, son, your daddy's here, your mother's here, and God's here. Now go to sleep!"

In a minute or two the little boy asked, "Daddy, was that God?"

A little boy was asked by a Sunday School teacher, "Who tore down the walls of Jericho?"

He said, "I didn't do it!"

The teacher was upset because he didn't know this Bible story, so she went to his mother and said, "I asked your son who tore down the walls of Jericho, and he answered me, 'I didn't do it.'"

His mother said, "Well, if he said he didn't do it, he didn't do it."

In exasperation, the teacher told his dad what the little boy had said. His dad blurted out, "Look, we don't want any trouble. How much did they cost?"

Another little boy was asked about Lot, Abraham's nephew in the Bible. He said that Lot's wife was a pillar of salt by day and a pillar of fire by night. It might have been the same little boy who was asked "Who was sorry when the prodigal returned home?" He replied, "the fatted calf."

———◆◇◆———

Sometimes young people do get it *almost* right, but just wrong enough to be funny. In a book called *Anguished English,* the author, Richard Lederer, said that these little nuggets had come from papers turned in by students:

"The government of England is a limited mockery."

"The English Navy defeated the Spanish armadillo."

"The Magna Carta declared that no free man could be hanged twice for the same offense."

"Anyone who has more than one wife is a pigamist."

"A bacteria is the back door of a cafeteria."

"When you breathe out you 'inspire.' If you don't breathe you 'expire.'"

"A fossil is an extinct animal. The older it is, the more extinct it is."

"Moses went up Mt. Cyanide and died. Solomon had 300 wives and 700 porcupines."

———◆◇◆———

One child writer said that Socrates went around

giving advice so they killed him. After his death, his career suffered a dramatic decline. And he said that Socrates died from an overdose of wedlock.

One little boy confessed to his Sunday School teacher, "I don't like being 'teachered.'"

The teacher corrected him, "It's not 'teachered,' it's 'taught.'"

He said, "I don't like being 'taughtered' either."

Several years back they discovered the Dead Sea Scrolls. A little boy overheard his parents talking about it and he said, "I sure hope they didn't find any more commandments."

A little boy about three or four years old kept standing up on the pew during church. His daddy would say, "Sit down!" And the little boy would stand up again. This went on until finally the father grabbed him by the shoulders and jammed him down in the pew and demanded, "I said, 'sit down.'"

The little boy looked up at his dad and said, "I may be sitting down *outside*, but *inside* I'm still standing up."

A lot of kids who go to school today know where and when the pilgrims landed, but sadly, they don't know why they ever sailed.

The kindergarten teacher had the kids singing "The Old Gray Mare." After they were finished singing, she asked the students, "Do you know what the old gray mare is?"

One of them said, "Yes, it's the man who runs the city."

———◆◆◆◆———

My dad kept a collection of things that kids said. Here are some of them:

H_2O is hot water; C_2O is cold water.

Arabs wear turbines on their heads.

To collect sulfur, hold a deacon over a flame in a test tube.

The three kinds of blood vessels are: arteries, veins, and caterpillars.

Rural life is mostly in the country.

The constitution was adopted to secure domestic hostility.

Beethoven was so deaf that he wrote loud music.

Lincoln was born in a log cabin that he built himself. And he wrote the emasculation proclamation.

Franklin invented electricity by rubbing two cats backwards.

Karl Marx became one of the Marx brothers.

———◆◆◆◆———

There were a couple of guys hauling garbage one windy day. Some of the paper they had picked up was blowing out of the truck. One of them said, "Let's stop the truck, and I'll get on top of the pile. He spread-eagled up there right on top of the paper to hold it down.

A woman and her little boy drove up behind them in her car. The little boy looked up at the garbage truck and said to his mother, "Hey, Momma, look there. Someone has thrown away a perfectly good man!"

Four boys were riding in a car together to school. They all had a test they didn't want to take, so they made up a lie to tell the teacher. They came in late and said they had a flat tire.

She replied, "Well, I'm going to let all of you make up the test. I want you to sit down, and I'm going to ask you just one question."

Relieved at having to answer only one question, the boys sat down and gave each other the thumbs up sign. The teacher handed them all a piece of paper and said, "Now, my question is: which tire was it that went flat?"

A kid was late for school on a cold winter morning and the teacher asked, "Why are you late?"

He said, "There was so much ice, I took one step forward and two backwards."

Perplexed, the teacher asked, "Then how did you get here?"

Proudly he said, "I turned around and walked home."

The following are creative answers that kids gave on tests:

In the Battle of Hastings, the angels and the Saxons were defeated by the Mormons.

Shakespeare wrote in Islamic pentameter.

A harp is a nude piano.

An equestrian is someone who asks questions.

A plagiarist is someone who writes plays.

A parasite is a kind of umbrella.

Amenable is anything that is mean.

An absentee ballot is when some are missing.

Bigotry is when a person is married to two or more women.

Husbandry is when a person has two or more husbands.

An octopus is an eye doctor.

A tycoon is something that butterflies come out of.

Molecules are so small, they can't be seen by a naked observer.

My friend was abducted into the National Honor Society.

The pope lives in a vacuum.

Marriage is also called "holy acrimony."

Heaven

One elderly gentleman passed away before his wife. He had requested that they write on his tomb, "Rest in peace," which they did, but his wife added under it, "until we meet again."

———◆❖◆———

Many years ago there was a man who survived the Jamestown flood—a very famous, devastating flood. Many times he was asked to give his testimony on how he survived. Finally, the man passed on and went to heaven where no one called on him to testify about it. Finally, he asked if he could give his testimony since he had done that so many times when he was down on the earth, and he thought everyone might be interested. They gave him a spot on the program—right after Noah.

———◆×◆———

There were two men who got killed in an accident late one Friday and went to heaven. They came up to the gate, and there was St. Peter who told them, "It's a little late to process you. The weekend is coming up so we'll have to do this on Monday."

Stunned, they asked, "Well, what will we do for the weekend?"

Peter said, "Well, you can do anything you want to do. We'll fix it up, and you can enjoy the weekend."

They asked, "Anything?"

Peter reassured them, "Yes, anything."

One of them said, "I've always wanted to be an eagle."

Peter said, "That's fine, and he released him."

The other one looked down at his shoes with great embarrassment. Peter said, "Well, what is it that you want to do?"

"Well," he said, "I'm too embarrassed."

Peter said, "Don't be embarrassed. What is it that you want to do?"

The fellow said, "Well, Peter, I've always wanted to be a stud."

Peter said, "That's fine," and he released him. As he walked over to the gate, his assistant asked, "What are they going to do this weekend?"

Peter said, "At this moment, one of them is soaring over the great Canadian Rockies."

He asked, "What about the other one?"

Peter said, "Well, he's holding up sheetrock down in Georgia."

One fellow found himself at the pearly gates. He was asked, "What are you doing here?"

He said, "Well, I shot myself in the foot."

He said, "That shouldn't have sent you up here."

The fellow said, "But my foot was in my mouth."

When the bishop died, his picture was placed in the paper over this caption: "Bishop Smith died yesterday. He had a clear vision of what the church wanted him to do."

Sports

A minister was getting ready to hit his golf ball over a lake. He put an old ball down for fear of losing it. He heard a voice inside that said, "Where is your faith—put down a new ball."

And so he decided to put down a new ball. Then he took a practice swing.

The voice spoke again saying, "Maybe you ought to put the old ball back down."

———◆✦◆———

Vince Lombardi said one time to his players, "If you're not fired with *enthusiasm*, some day you will be *fired* with enthusiasm.

———◆✦◆———

We live in a time when people are very sensitive and easily offended. There was a woman who was so sensitive that when she attended a football game and the players gathered in a huddle, she thought they were talking about her.

———◆✦◆———

There was a man and his wife who had a brand new baby. They brought it home from the hospital, and he decided to weigh it on the same scales that he weighed his fish on. The baby weighed 33 pounds.

Dad

I ministered for many years with a great man of God named Ern Baxter. Ern passed away in 1993 and is with the Lord. But he was a very eloquent orator from the old school. He could paint great word pictures and had a broad vocabulary. Ern and I knew each other several years before he met my father.

Now my father was more of a straightforward, country preacher. Dad was a good preacher and could be eloquent when he wanted to, but he was more down to earth and preached to rural folks most of his life. When Ern met him, he wanted to impress upon my father how much he thought of me. Now my dad and my mom always loved me, I didn't doubt that, but I never felt they were overly impressed with me. Ern was trying to tell my father what a wonderful person I was. I knew that just any minute my dad was going to say something down to earth and straightforward, but I was curious as to what it would be.

As Ern waxed eloquent about me to my father who knew me far better, my dad couldn't take it any longer and interrupted him, saying, "That's fine, Brother Baxter, but if it wasn't for the grace of God, Charles would be in hell right now." He and I both laughed although Ern seemed a little stunned by it. It was exactly the truth.

———————

Back in the early 1930s, my father was pastor of a church where he had some problems, so he decided to resign. A fellow minister in the town who was older gave him some good advice. He said, "Vernon, you don't need to defend yourself in all of this. Your enemies won't believe it and your friends don't need it."

That advice impressed me because people who love you don't need to hear you defend yourself, and people who don't love you won't believe it when you do.

My father passed away right near the age of 86 and kept his sense of humor right up until the end. But he used to say to me, "Son, old age is not for sissies." He also used to say to me something that was very wise, "The happiest people in the world are those who live for something besides themselves."

Preaching

There was a minister who was fond of quoting a verse of Scripture for everything that happened. He was preaching along one night and a fly flew right into his open mouth. He paused a moment, looked at the congregation and said, "He was a stranger, and I took him in."

Somebody once said that a religious awakening is what happens when the preacher quits preaching.

One Vermont farmer listened to a preacher give a long-winded sermon. As he went out the door, he said, "Young man, it's always a good thing to turn loose of the handle when you finish pumping."

Preaching in some churches is like a dog chasing a parked car. He can make a lot of racket, but nothing's going anywhere.

Aging

Recently I read about the prayer of *senility*. Of course, you have heard about the prayer of serenity. The prayer of senility goes like this: Lord, help me to forget the people that I never liked, the good fortune to run into the ones that I do, and the eyesight to be able to tell the difference.

An old gent cut his finger, and his wife suggested that he go to the clinic down the street. And so he went in the front door. There were two doors in the lobby. One marked, "over 65" and the other marked, "under 65."

So being a senior citizen, he went through the door marked "over 65" only to be met by two more doors. One said, "internal" and the other said, "external."

He figured, "well, it's external." So he went through that door only to be met by two more doors. One said, "male" and the other said "female."

So he went through the door marked "male" only to be met by two more doors. One said "major," and the other said, "minor."

So he thought, "This is minor." So he went through the door marked "minor" only to find himself back out on the street.

Perplexed, he went on back home. His wife said, "Honey, did they help you?"

"No," he said, "but they sure were organized."

There was an elderly couple in bed one night. The old gentleman was about to go to sleep when his wife said to him, "Honey, you don't love me any more."

He asked, "Why do you say that?"

She said, "Well, you used to hug me more than you do now."

So he rolled over, gave her a big hug, and rolled back over and started to go to sleep.

After a moment, she said, "You know, you used to tell me that you loved me."

So he said, "Well, I love you." And he thought that would do.

A few minutes later, she still hadn't gone to sleep so she said, "This may sound silly, but you used to nibble me on the ear." Whereupon the old gentleman got out of bed. She asked, "Where are you going?"

He said, "I'm going to the bathroom to get my teeth."

Three old gentlemen were talking about the problems of age. One of them said to the other, "You know, sometimes I am driving somewhere and forget where I'm going."

The other one said, "I know exactly what you mean. I can call somebody on the phone and forget who I'm calling."

The third one said, "Well, I'm glad I don't have that problem, knock on wood." He knocked on the table, and he said, "Uh-oh, somebody's at the door."

You know you're getting old...

...when you sink your teeth into a thick steak, and they stay there.

...when you feel like it's the morning after, and you didn't go anywhere the night before.

... when you look forward to a dull evening.

...when a little old lady helps you across the street, and it's your wife.

…when you get winded playing chess.

…when everything that doesn't hurt doesn't work.

…when the gleam in your eyes is the sun hitting your bifocals.

…when your children are older than you remember your parents being when you were young.

…when your mind makes contracts that your body can't keep.

…when you finally know all the answers, and nobody's asking you any questions.

…when the favorite part of the newspaper is the section under the heading "25 years ago today."

…when you sit down in a rocking chair and can't get it going.

…when your knees buckle but your belt won't.

…when your back goes out more often than you do.

…when you get excited and your pacemaker makes the garage door go up.

…when your house is too big, and the medicine cabinet is too small.

…when you wake up and realize that the best part of the day is over.

…when you figure that if God wanted you to touch your toes, He would have put them on your knees.

…when your spouse says, "Let's go upstairs and make love," and you say, "Honey, we can't do both."

…when your friends compliment you on your new alligator shoes, and you're not wearing shoes.

74

An old executive was retiring and the young executive who was going to take his place asked him, "What is the secret of your success?"

The old man thought a little bit and said, "Well, I guess good decisions."

He asked, "Well how do you make good decisions?"

The old executive thought a moment and said, "I guess experience."

"Well, how do you get experience?"

The old man looked at him and said, "Bad decisions."

My friend Charles Green told me this story: A man went over to his elderly neighbor who was sitting on the front porch late one evening and asked, "George, what did y'all do this evening?"

George thought a minute and said, "We went to a movie."

He said, "What did you see?"

George went blank and in a few minutes he began to gesture. He said, "Flower, pretty flower. Red. Pretty flower."

The man asked, "Rose?"

George said, "Yes."

The old gentleman hollered to his wife, "Rose, what did we see at the movies tonight?"

A number of years ago, I heard Jack Hayford speak at a minister's conference after a recent birthday when he had received a number of cards. He described some of the cards.

One of them said: "At your age you've got a lot going for you: Your knees are going, your back is going, your hair is going, and your teeth are going…"

Another card said: "This card is so funny that your hair will fall out." You open the card, and it says, "Oh, I see you have already heard it."

Another one said: "You're not the only person celebrating your 29th birthday today, but you certainly are the oldest."

The final one showed a little old man sitting among a lot of presents. The card read, "Is that you sitting among your presents or did someone give you an old person for your birthday?"

A 65-year-old woman had a baby, and her older daughter came over to see it. The mother said, "You can't see it until it cries."

And her daughter asked, "Why? I'm not going to wake it up, I just want to see it."

And she said, "I'm sorry, you can't see it until it cries."

But her daughter insisted.

So finally the mother said, "Look, I *forgot* where I put it. So you can't see it till it cries."

An old gentleman who was still a good golfer, but who couldn't see very well, invited another retiree who had good vision to play with him. On the first tee, he struck the ball very well but soon it was out of his sight. He asked his friend, "Did you see the ball?"

Confidently he replied, "Yes."

He asked, "Where did it go?"

After thinking for a minute his friend confessed, "I forgot!"

Folks

People in the South have been known for sayings or metaphors that communicate a truth. Sometimes they can be very funny. For example, my dad used to say that someone was "smiling like a mule eating briers."

———❖———

Another friend, Garland Pemberton, said that it was so dark, it was as dark as the inside of a mule.

———❖———

My barber, Chris, said that a man had so much money he could burn up a wet mule with one dollar bills.

———❖———

Other sayings:
"The man who is rowing the boat doesn't have time to rock it."
"Prejudice is being down on what you're not up on."
"For a speech to be any good, it had to be an improvement on silence."
"A man ate so much boiled okra he couldn't keep his socks up."
"A minute of silence can prevent an hour of explanation."

"He always aimed to tell the truth, but he was a very poor marksman."

"A foolish man is always waiting for his ship to come in, even though he never sends one out."

A farmer witnessed an accident next to his property. The police asked him who he thought was in the wrong. He said, "Well, they hit each other about the same time."

A well-dressed driver of a fine car stopped to ask a farmer leaning over a fence, "Can you tell me how to get back to the state highway?"

The farmer put his thumbs through his overalls, looked thoughtful, and said, "I can't tell you for sure."

He asked, "Well, can you tell me how far it is to the nearest town?"

Stroking his cheek, the farmer replied, "No, I can't rightly say."

Finally, in exasperation, the fellow shouted, "Well you don't know anything, do you?"

The farmer drawled, "Well, I ain't lost."

———◆◆◆◆———

Sometimes when you try to do things you get a lot of criticism. My wife shared with me a quote that she read, "The loudest boos always come from the cheap seats."

———◆◆◆◆———

There was a small town in the rural South with a young public defender. His first case was a chicken thief. The public defender went to court and argued strenuously on behalf of his client and got him off.

As they were walking out of the courthouse, his client said to him, "Does that mean I get to keep the chicken?"

———◆◆◆◆———

One of the funniest books I ever read was a book entitled, *Curing the Cross-Eyed Mule* by Loyal Jones and Billy Edd Wheeler. Let me say, I wouldn't endorse all the stories in it, but it faithfully depicts a certain culture in rural America. One of the stories is about a farmer who went to a neighboring farm and asked his friend about his mule. He said, "I heard your mule got sick. Mine is sick now, too. What did you give him?"

His neighbor answered, "Turpentine."

So the farmer went home and gave his mule turpentine, and it died. He angrily marched back to his farmer friend and demanded, "I thought you said you gave your mule turpentine."

He said, "I did."

"Well, I gave mine turpentine, and he died."

The other farmer said, "Yep. Mine did, too."

Which proves if you're going to ask a farmer a question, you'd better ask him the right question because he may not tell you anymore than you ask for.

America is beset by polls. We have polls and surveys for everything. One Sunday afternoon a pollster called a man and woke him up from a good nap. The man was in a bad mood. The pollster asked him, "What do you think is America's greatest problem? Ignorance or apathy?

The man said, "I don't know, and I don't care!"

The path of least resistance makes men and rivers crooked.

You can't drift your way to success.

Anxiety will not help the future, but it sure will ruin the present.

Anger is a strong wind that blows out the light of reason.

If you're one step ahead, you're a leader; if you're two steps ahead, you're a pioneer; if you're three steps ahead, you're a martyr.

If you're too big to be led, you're too little to lead.

If you don't know where you are going, any road will get you there.

———◆◆◆◆◆———

The Church used to be a thermostat that affected the temperature in the world. Now it's just a thermometer that reflects it.

Casual Christians become Christian casualties.

One of the hardest things to do is to get off a high horse gracefully.

You can't soar with the eagles if you're hooting with the owls.

A camel is a racehorse put together by a committee.

A bumper sticker said, "Give me ambiguity or give me something else."

Someone said we like to judge ourselves by our *intentions*, while we judge others by their *actions*.

———◆◆◆◆◆———

I was speaking at a church years ago in a rural area of southern Louisiana. One of the men there told me, "You know a lot of people are educated way beyond their intelligence."

Famous Folks

Winston Churchill was a very wise man, and there are many wonderful quotes attributed to him. One is, "If we open a quarrel with the past, we will lose the future." He said that at the beginning of World War II, it would have been easy to blame his fellow Englishmen for their failure to arm and prepare for the war. Instead he decided to welcome them into the preparation without condemning them for their past failure. That's a great lesson in forgiveness and in wisdom. We need everyone in the struggle against evil.

He also said, "Men occasionally stumble on the truth, but they always manage to pick themselves up and carry on as if nothing happened."

———◆◆◆◆———

My friend, Don Basham, with whom I ministered for many years, used to say, "After all is said and done, there's more said than done."

———◆◆◆◆———

Billy Graham once said, "If you aim at nothing, you will hit it."

———◆◆◆◆———

Oral Roberts said, "Anyone can learn to preach, but only God can give you a testimony." Another time he said, "I am going to preach like a fat man going through a barbed wire fence. I will touch on a couple of points and pass on."

———◆◆◆◆———

Dr. R.G. Lee said in a sermon one time that a man had a tongue so long he could sit on the front porch and lick the skillet.

One of my favorite sayings is by Les Brown, an African-American motivational speaker: "Methods are many; principles are few. Methods always change, but principles never do." That's why, as a minister, I like to teach on principles because principles are not prejudiced, they work for everybody.

Another one from Les: "Adversity introduces a man to himself." And: "Wherever you find yourself, remember you made an appointment to be there."

He also said, "The paper says that millions of people are dying because of what they're eating. But I'm telling you that millions of people are dying because of what's eating them."

———◆◆◆———

Bill Cosby was asked what is the secret of success. He said, "I don't know, but the secret of failure is trying to please everybody."

———◆◆◆———

George Lui, chairman of the President's Baking Company said, "Some people will just quit and leave. That's okay. But others will quit and stay, and that's bad. It's not acceptable."

———◆◆◆———

Jim Rohn, who is another favorite teacher of mine, said that concerning success, "People who can't see it for themselves, certainly can't see it for you."

Jim also said, "Let the past teach you, not beat you." And, "If the promise is clear, the price is easy."

When he was given a great introduction followed by applause, he said, "I'll tell you what the cow said to the farmer on a cold morning. 'Thanks for the warm hand.'"

Dennis Waitely was speaking of how we think. He said, "The software drives the hardware, and the mind drives the body."

Victor Frankl observed while he was in prison during World War II that the people who were willing to share their last piece of bread lived longer during the holocaust.

Arnold Toynbee said, "Civilizations die of suicide, not murder."

Someone asked Abraham Lincoln if you called a dog's tail a leg, how many legs does the dog have? He said, "Only four. Calling the tail a leg doesn't make it one."

Helen Keller said, "The only thing worse than losing your sight is losing your vision."

Benjamin Franklin said, "I'd rather hear someone say, 'Well done!' than to hear someone say, 'Well said.'"

Mr. Joske who founded the famous department store chain said, "Vision without task is fantasy. Task without vision is drudgery."

Lyndon Johnson was given a great introduction to which he responded, "My father would have loved it and my mother would have believed it."

Norman Cousins once was given such a great introduction, he said, "Now would be a good time to die."

Beliefs

When I was young, nobody ever heard of the New Age Movement. Now at the turn of the century, it has become rather popular. Of course, it's not new; it's just a new name. The New Age movement is the modern equivalent of witch doctors. It is a tour through the swamp of subjectivism. I heard Shirley MacLaine interviewed on Larry King Live once, and she stated, "You can create your own reality." I thought, *Now that won't work if you're on a railroad track.*

A friend of mine named Bryn Jones said that theology has become *feelology*. That's a profound statement because we think reality is how we feel. A lot of people feel *good* because they haven't read today's mail. Some people feel *bad* because they haven't read some promise from God. Feelings can be deceptive, but they seem to dominate today's world. I expect to get on an airplane one day and have the pilot come on and say, "I *feel* like we're flying north. How do all of you *feel* about it? The stewardess will be passing down the aisle with a questionnaire and would you please fill it out. We would like to know how all of you *feel* about it." I think I would say I feel like we need to get this plane down on the ground. If he doesn't have a compass and some good electronics that tell him what reality is, I don't want to fly with him. I don't want to fly with anybody that gets *feelings* mixed up with *reality*.

That reminds me of something Victor Frankl said while imprisoned in Germany during WWII: "The last freedom a person has is the freedom to determine his attitude in any given situation." He also said that America needs a second statue. "The U.S. has the Statue of Liberty on the east coast; we need a statue of responsibility. I suggest that we put that on the west coast. In fact, I suggest that we put it on Alcatraz to remind people of what happens when they use their liberty without responsibility."

I heard someone else say, "Most people are not really against you—they just don't care."

———◆◆◆◆◆———

The following is a quote taken from a speech given by Theodore Roosevelt at Sorbonne in 1910. My wife had it framed for me:

"It's not the critic who counts. It's not the one who points out how the strong man stumbles or where the doer of deeds could have done them better. The credit belongs to the man who is actually in the arena, whose face is marred by dust and sweat and blood, who strives valiantly, who errs and comes short again and again because there is no effort without error and shortcoming but who does actually strive to do the deeds, who knows the great enthusiasms, the great devotions, who spends himself in a worthy cause, who at the best at the end knows the triumphs of achievement and who at the worst if he fails at least fails while daring greatly so that his place shall never be with those cold and timid souls who know neither victory nor defeat."

That is a very powerful statement to our society that has become more and more a spectator society, a commentating society, and too often a critical society. All the while we *do* less for ourselves.

———◆◆◆◆◆———

I heard one minister say years ago that we had analysis of paralysis. Someone else has said that the critic is the person who goes up after the battle and shoots all the wounded. Someone else said that the only people who are not bothered by critics are those who *do* nothing, who *say* nothing, and who *are* nothing.

———◆◆◆◆◆———

For years, communism was the big threat to the western world. Communism, of course, was fundamentally atheistic. It was an attempt to rule without God.

In 1991, the Soviet flag was lowered for the last time on Christmas night. How ironic. The Bible says, "The fool has said in his heart there is no God." The first wise atheist has yet to be born. Some people thought that Karl Marx was one, but indeed he was not. In fact, he was foolish enough to be indirectly responsible for the deaths of more people than any other single person in history. The Person he denied brought salvation to more people than any other person in history. Christ is not only the Alpha, He is also the Omega and He will still be Lord when every other name has bowed before Him.

———◆◆◆◆◆———

Norman Snaith observed in his book, *The Distinctive Ideas of the Old Testament,* that the ancient Greeks focused on knowing *self,* and that the ancient Hebrews focused on knowing *God.* That's the difference between a society that survives, and one that doesn't.

Someone said that the two most important days in our lives is the day we're born and the day we find out why. A lot of people never have experienced the second day.

Friends

My friend Ern Baxter told a story about a contest that happened many years ago when boys were called upon to ride their bicycles down a narrow plank. The one who was able to do that would win a prize. All the boys fells off, except one who made it all the way to the end. After the contest was over, the judge asked him, "How were you able to do it?"

He replied, "Well everybody else was looking at the plank or their front wheel. I was looking at the end of the plank."

If you're going to succeed, you have to keep your eyes on the goal and not on the situation.

Another time Ern said, "If Columbus had turned back, no one would have blamed him. But then, no one would have remembered him either."

My friend Houston Miles, a pastor in South Carolina, defined a fanatic as "someone who redoubles his effort after he's lost his sense of direction." He also said, "Man is the only creature, when patted on the back, his head begins to swell."

My friend John Duke said, "We're often praying that God will give the world to us, but He cannot until He gives us to the world."

My friend Charles Green was preaching about the wilderness experience that Israel endured and similar experiences we all seem to have. He gave an excellent piece of advice: "Don't make a permanent mistake in a temporary wilderness."

My friend Gary Henley who heads International Outreach Ministries said, "Bitterness is like drinking poison and waiting for the other guy to die."

My friend Robert Grant told me a quote by Wayne Gretsky, the great hockey player. When asked what was the secret of his success, he said, "The key is not to skate to where the puck *is*, but to skate to where the puck *will be*."

That is a very clever answer. A lot of people are skating to where it is now. Others are skating to where it has never been nor will be. They are just skating.

———◆·◆◆·◆———

My father-in-law, Dr. Albert Dix, wrote a book of humor entitled, *Humor: The Bright Side of Pain*. It was a book of sayings that he collected over the years as a physician. People would say some very funny things to him. One of the things a patient said to him was, "As you know, doctor, the Bible says that a lie is an abomination to the Lord and an ever present help in a time of need."

———◆·◆◆·◆———

My friend John Norwood, who recently passed on, shared with me many humorous stories over the years. He once shared with me parts of letters actually received by the Welfare Department when people were applying for support:

• "I cannot get sick pay. I have six children. Can you tell me why?"
• "Please find for certain if my husband is dead. The man I am now living with can't eat or do anything until he knows."
• "I am very much annoyed to find that you have branded my son illiterate. This is a dirty lie as I was married a week before he was born."
• "You have changed my little boy to a girl. Will this make any difference?"

95

And John also shared a story about an elderly gentleman who lived in El Dorado, Arkansas. The man was a very unpretentious man, with little formal education, but who had been very successful in business.

In the early 1960s, he and his wife decided it was time for them to enjoy themselves by traveling. So they decided to begin by taking a trip out west. Having never driven on an interstate highway before, the man was not accustomed to the fast pace of traffic on the Los Angeles freeways. He was driving along on one at 40 mph, and all of the other cars were blowing their horns at him and passing his car at high rates of speed. Finally a state trooper pulled him over so he could inform him that the minimum speed was 50 mph.

When the trooper walked up to his car, he said to the man from Arkansas, "I guess you know why I am stopping you..."

To which the gentleman replied, "Yeah, I'm the only one out here you can catch!"

Humor

Norman Cousins is a well-know humorist. He became a professor at a university in California and for
years he was a successful business executive. An article
he wrote, entitled, "I Laughed My Way to Health," impressed me very much. It seems that he was extremely
ill with some kind of disease that made his skin so sen-

sitive he couldn't stand for it to be touched. He was in the hospital for quite a while and wasn't getting any better. He decided to check himself out into a hotel next to the hospital as an outpatient. Some friends of his brought some funny movies over and he watched them. They were very funny, and he found himself laughing as hard as he had ever laughed. He noticed that when he laughed really hard that the pain would go away for up to 30 minutes. And so he decided to get all the funny material that he could and just have one big laugh marathon, which he did. Eventually he was cured. It was discovered later that when you laugh, your body releases some morphinous-like substances inside that are natural painkillers.

Laughter indeed is a good medicine. Victor Borge once said that the shortest distance between two people is laughter.

I hope you have enjoyed the stories in this book, and I hope it made you laugh a time or two. Share laughter with a friend or neighbor today and watch what it can do!

ABOUT THE AUTHOR

Charles Simpson is an internationally-known author, Bible teacher, motivational speaker, and pastor, who has been in ministry since 1955. His humor and story-telling often carry a deeper message that is prophetic in its *timeliness* and *timelessness*.

Born in New Orleans in 1937, Charles grew up as the son of a Baptist pastor in southern Louisiana, and then later in southern Alabama. In 1964, he and his church were swept up in what became known as the Charismatic Renewal movement. He became a pioneer and leader in that movement, traveling around the world and teaching thousands of people. In 1969, he became part of the founding Editorial Board of *New Wine* Magazine, an international publication dedicated to Christian growth. Other notable Bible teachers associated with *New Wine* include Don Basham, Ern Baxter, Bob Mumford, and Derek Prince.

In 1973, Charles and a team of pastors founded Covenant Church of Mobile, Alabama, on the concept of small house fellowship groups, dedicated to building strong organic relationships—not only among Christians—but also reaching out to family, friends, neighbors, and co-workers with the love and Good News of Jesus Christ. This church also had a strong emphasis on praise and worship. In 1985, Covenant Church and *New Wine* gave birth to Integrity Music, which is now the largest praise and worship music company in the world.

New Wine ceased publication in 1986, and Charles launched a publication that is known today as *One-to-*

One Magazine, which focuses on "Extending the kingdom of God...one person at a time." Charles continues to serve as Editor-in-Chief of this magazine, and is a featured writer in every issue. Under the banner of CSM Publishing, *One-to-One* and its related website, tapes, books, videos, and letters now reach more than 70 nations worldwide.

Charles is the author of numerous books, including *Courageous Living* and *The Challenge to Care*, and he was the Senior Editor of *The Covenant & the Kingdom* Bible study curriculum. Charles served as a contributor to the commentary for the popular *Spirit-Filled Life Bible*.

He has logged literally millions of miles of travel, sharing the Gospel of Christ's Kingdom and ministering across the globe. Charles resides with his wife, Carolyn, in the Mobile area. They have three adult children and two grandchildren.

CHARLES SIMPSON MINISTRIES

Charles Simpson Ministries (CSM) sends out thousands of pieces of literature every month to every corner of the earth...in fact, to more than 70 nations. Charles' writings have been translated into many languages, including Spanish, Russian, Mandarin Chinese, Telegu (India), Slovak, Polish, Swedish, and more.

The mission of CSM is to equip and encourage believers to share their faith with others in word and deed. Some of the ways in which we fulfill this mission include:

• *One-to-One* **Magazine** – an award-winning quarterly that features encouraging testimonies, news, and practical Bible teaching with a prophetic edge.

• **Pastoral Letter from Charles Simpson** – a fresh monthly message straight from Charles' heart to you.

• **www.csmpublishing.org** – a regularly-updated website filled with photos, ministry updates, and perspective on world events, as well as a ministry store stocked with vital encouraging and equipping resources for you, your church, and your neighbors.

• **Audio Tapes and Videos** – Experience the warmth, humor, and dynamic teaching of Charles Simpson captured "live" and delivered to you and your friends.

• *The Covenant & the Kingdom* – a comprehensive, systematic, user-friendly Bible study curriculum.

• *Conquista Cristiana* – our Spanish language publication edited by Hugo Zelaya, and reaching key leaders across the Americas and Europe.

• **Costa Rica Children's Outreach** – a ministry led by Enrique and Charlyn Mejia, the son-in-law and daughter of Charles and Carolyn Simpson, providing foster care, feeding, shelter, medical attention…and lots of love…to desperately needy children in the San José area.

• **International Outreach Ministries** – under the direction of Gary Henley, this ministry, founded in 1986 by Paul Petrie, serves missionaries on every continent, as well as educating and motivating Christians on issues of key concern, and marshalling resources to meet critical needs.

Charles Simpson personally travels and ministers across the United States, as do Gary Henley, *One-to-One* Editor Stephen Simpson, and CSM associated Evangelists Ronald Gray and Jim Newsom. For booking information, contact CSM.

CSM
Publishing and International Outreach
P.O. Box Z
Mobile, AL 36616